WRITE

· WITH ·

CONQUER WRITER'S BLOCK, UNLEASH
YOUR CREATIVITY, AND WRITE YOUR
BOOK USING ARTIFICIAL INTELLIGENCE

"Rob is one the kings of helping people get the idea of the book out of their minds onto pages and into the marketplace."
- Russell Brunson

WRITE

 WITH

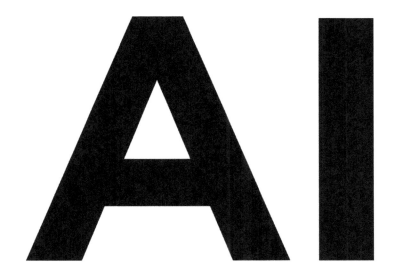

CONQUER WRITER'S BLOCK, UNLEASH YOUR CREATIVITY, AND WRITE YOUR BOOK USING ARTIFICIAL INTELLIGENCE

ROB KOSBERG

AUTHOR OF THE WALL STREET JOURNAL BESTSELLER, PUBLISH. PROMOTE. PROFIT.™

A GIFT FOR YOU!

Discover how **Write with AI** can transform your writing and move you from stuck to complete in a matter of days.

We have a **Special Bonus Video** for the readers of this book that you don't want to miss. It will take you through everything you need to know to start writing your book with the help of AI.

publishmybestseller.com/ai-workshop

But wait, there's more!

Also get this **FREE BONUS:** Get booked on TV, Radio, and other media (a $997 value)

It includes video training, TV segment proposal template, example booking script, and the top 100 radio and TV contact list.

It's all yours for **FREE** with this book!

DON'T WAIT

Watch this **FREE VIDEO TRAINING** and learn how YOU can become the **HUNTED!**

www.publishpromoteprofit.com/free

Published by Best Seller Publishing®, St. Augustine, FL
Best Seller Publishing® is a registered trademark.
Printed in the United States of America.
ISBN: 978-1-962595-38-4

For more information, please write:
Best Seller Publishing®
1775 US-1 #1070
St. Augustine, FL 32084
or call 1 (626) 765-9750

Visit us online at:
www.BestSellerPublishing.org

TABLE OF CONTENTS

PRAISE FOR ROB AND BEST SELLER PUBLISHING

Travis King

Best Seller Publishing is legit! I decided that Best Seller Publishing was the publisher I wanted to work with, not only to bring my book to life but also to intelligently launch it, … More

Ruben Narvaez Garcia

Rob and all of his staff at Best Seller Publishing are amazing! Everyone was very professional and very detailed in everything they did. I am very grateful for their service and support. My book is a #1 International Best Seller in 11 countries!

Michael Kublin

I can't thank my team at BSP enough. Working with Coach Matt was a fabulous experience as he guided me every step of the way. From start to finish, Bob and his team of experienced experts made my book publishing simple and a tremendous pleasure. Thank you all so very much.

Heather Dunlop
★ ★ ★ ★ ★

What an incredible experience! I had wanted to write my book for 2 years. I kept wanting to add more and more info, and change the layout, and was spinning in circles. I was tired of having the book in my head and not getting anywhere. I got all of that resolved with Rob and his team.

Shauneille Smith
★ ★ ★ ★ ★

BSP consistently fulfilled its commitments, maintaining a high level of professionalism throughout the entire process. The knowledgeable BSP team, well-versed in the industry, has significantly facilitated the placement of my book in various bookstores.

Ben Moss
★ ★ ★ ★ ★

BSP was recommended to me by a friend who had written a book and used BSP to help guide him through the process. In my case, I wrote the text and approached BSP once I was ready to start the self-publishing process. From start to finish, they were extremely helpful.

Dr. Atousa Mahdavi
★ ★ ★ ★ ★

I have been a client of BSP and my book Wholly You became a best seller as they promised. Aside from that, I have loved working with the team. They are very understanding of the author's demands for perfection and work with you to make that happen. I highly recommend BSP!

Denis Lamoureux
★ ★ ★ ★ ★

I had a fabulous experience working with Best Seller Publishing. Over my 25 years of professional articles and books, it has always frustrated me that publishers do not often listen to the authors. In sharp contrast, BSP listened carefully to my needs.

Denise Stegall
★ ★ ★ ★ ★

Wow, what a great experience! Working With Best Seller Publishing has been an amazing journey and it's not over yet. Writing my book with the support of my editor made what seemed a tough task a truly enjoyable process. The words flowed easily.

Cassandra Houston
★ ★ ★ ★ ★

This journey with Best Seller Publishing has been the best journey ever. I just made Best Selling Author not only nationally but internationally. When they guarantee making you a best seller, they keep to their word. They are engaged with you every step of the way.

George Jackson Jr
★ ★ ★ ★ ★

Best Seller Publishing over-delivered! They provide an excellent platform for new and experienced authors to obtain the credibility of a best-seller ranking in a "done for you" fashion with amazing results.

Marc Nolan
★ ★ ★ ★ ★

Rob and the entire BSP team have been AWESOME to work with on my book. I've written two others using another Publisher and they were not even close to Rob and his team.

Tonya Mikelson
★ ★ ★ ★ ★

I am a first-time writer and was very nervous about investing money into something I didn't have complete confidence in my skill level on, but their training helped me a ton and gave me more confidence while I was writing.

Roane Hunter
★ ★ ★ ★ ★

The entire process with BSP has been a great experience! Each member of the team was very responsive, professional, and knowledgeable. Our book achieved Best Seller status as promised and we could not be more appreciative of their support in this entire endeavor! BSP delivers results - we highly recommend them!

LaQuanda Evans
★ ★ ★ ★ ★

From start to finish the BSP team has been amazing. They have become part of my family. I'm working with them on another book. I definitely recommend them. Invest in yourself and the outcome will be much greater with BSP on your side!

Pradeep Kumar ★ ★ ★ ★ ★

It was a great experience working with BSP. The whole team was very supportive and cooperative and paid great attention to detail. The experience made us feel as if it was more like their own baby much more than it was ours.

Jim Riviello ★ ★ ★ ★ ★

Rob Kosberg and his team are simply the best. The entire experience from the first call to best-seller status has been absolutely great. The BSP team takes the time to outline a plan and assign the right specialist depending on the phase of the book. Highly recommend!

INTRODUCTION

*I love deadlines. I love the whooshing noise they
make as they go by.*

– Douglas Adams

Y ou've been wanting to write a book for a long time, haven't you? At Best Seller Publishing, we've helped thousands of clients write their book, launch it to bestseller status, use it to get on TV, radio, and in the media, and make a huge income and impact with it. One thing we've found is that the average client (usually a very successful person in their field) who comes to us has been wanting to write their book for more than five years.

You're not alone in this. A survey done by *The New York Times* about 15 years ago found that 81% of all Americans want to write a book. The problem is, less than 1% ever actually accomplish it. It is so difficult to do with so many different directions to go in. Many people want to write their life stories, pass on their wisdom, and share their knowledge.

Others want to write books, similar to my last book, *Publish. Promote. Profit.*, a *Wall Street Journal* bestseller, to use that book to attract clients, get speaking engagements, and build credibility in their marketplace.

Just last week, one of my clients messaged me excitedly to share that she'd just finished up her TED Talk and it went fantastically. She's been on dozens of TV shows and speaking engagements and she told me she was just reached out to by *The Drew Barrymore Show* because they saw her book and they want to have her on as well. Her entire profile of authority and credibility is exploding, all because of her book. Who doesn't want that? After all, we are in this to make as big of an impact as we can, aren't we?

Imagine if I told you that by doing just one thing, you could significantly increase your chances of doubling, or even tripling, your current income? That one transformative action? Writing your own book. A survey conducted among entrepreneurs who have published a book revealed that 34% of thousands of respondents reported their income had doubled since their book's publication. I can personally attest to this phenomenon. The publication of my first book, about 15 years ago, grew my income tenfold in the very first year!

Welcome to *Write with AI*, a step by step guide that I believe will transform your writing process and help you finally write your first book or revolutionize your writing and massively speed up your content creation process. This book is designed to introduce you to the Manuscriptr Method, a unique approach that leverages the power of artificial intelligence to unlock your creativity and set your writing free.

You see, a book can change everything for you.

John Maxwell, the famous leadership expert, wrote his first book in 1979. A book you have probably never heard of, entitled *Think On These Things*. John's first book didn't do very well. In fact, it was six years before he wrote his second book in 1985. Somewhere down the line, John figured it out, though. By the '90s, John was writing as many as six books per year and his credibility and authority were exploding.

Today, John has 70 titles in print and has sold over 20 million books. We know him as a world-famous leadership expert because of all the books and his speaking career. Did he achieve it with his first book? No, but clearly something changed in John, and he learned to be incredibly prolific. John went from being a small-church preacher to the foremost leadership expert in the world, commanding $100,000 speaking fees, impacting millions of lives, and earning millions of dollars in revenue and income. He figured it out. I believe this can help you figure it out as well.

By the way, it may be a mistake using somebody like John Maxwell as an example. You see, you think of John Maxwell as the world-famous leadership expert and author. You should be thinking of John Maxwell as the guy who wrote his first book in 1979 that didn't do very well, because that's the stage that many of you are at right now.

You see, before John Maxwell was the John Maxwell we know of today, he was the John Maxwell of 1979, who had never written a book. Eventually, he would go on to write 70 books and sell 20 million copies of his books. There is no reason that you can't do the exact same thing he did. So, stop thinking of him, or any other guru, in their present state. Think of them instead as the person that, just like you, had to start writing, just like you have to start without knowing where this will actually end up.

You see, every first-time (and seventieth-time) author faces similar problems and challenges.

Problem: 81% of people want to write a book, but less than 1% succeed. The 1% must be better, smarter, and sexier than the rest of us.

Answer: WRONG. Successful authors are no different than unsuccessful ones. They just have a better process and map to achieve their goal of writing. Maybe the finished book does make them sexier, though!

Problem: The average nonfiction e-book sells 250 copies in its lifetime, so why does it even matter if that is the likelihood?

Answer: Well that's an awfully negative way to approach this! It is true, though, so you'd better have a good plan to ensure your book stands out and is successfully marketed. Don't worry, I have some things that will help you out.

Problem: I am not sure WHO I am writing for or what my audience actually wants.

Answer: This one is not nearly as hard but unfortunately most authors never get around to researching it. Zig Ziglar used to say, "We're all listening to the same radio station: WIIFM. What's in it for me?" That's what your readers want to know when they look at the title of your book, when they look at the cover of your book, and when they look at your table of contents. They want to know, "What is in it for me?" And you should ask that question before you ever start writing.

Problem: I am not even sure why I am writing a book, let alone if I want to write many books!

Answer: I hate to say it, but YOU are going to have to answer this one. Not knowing your why is a BIG problem. I know mine. At this point, I write for my businesses. I am very pragmatic and honest with my clients. Yes, I want to create something important. Yes, I want to create something good. Even VERY good. But... I write to grow my business and help other writers grow theirs. If the good Lord gives me more time on this earth, I will write more for my kids and future generations. For now, it's all business, baby. What about you?

Look, obviously, I don't know why you're interested in writing a book. Maybe you've been told by other people that you need to tell your story. They listen to you and think, "Wow, your life should be a book." Awesome.

Maybe you're just curious and wondering, "I've always felt like I wanted to write a book, and perhaps this can help me to do it." Well, it certainly can. Maybe you really want to help other people and you know that your story, and what you've overcome, could make a massive difference in somebody else's life.

Perhaps you're just like me: you have a business, you have clients you love to serve, and you absolutely know that a book will help you to explode your income and your impact on the world. Bravo. It certainly did mine. Maybe you actually just want to start a business using a book. A book is an awesome way to pivot

Harness the power of AI to overcome your writer's block, lack of inspiration, or the daunting task of structuring your book for ease of writing and content creation.

and transition into a brand-new career. That's exactly what happened with me.

This book will show you how to harness the power of AI to overcome your writer's block, lack of inspiration, or the daunting task of structuring your book for ease of writing and content creation. It will guide you on how to use AI as a tool to stimulate your imagination, generate ideas, and even draft sections of your book. Whether you're a seasoned author or a first timer, this book and Manuscriptr will open up a new world of possibilities, making the writing process more enjoyable and a lot less stressful.

So, are you ready to get this going and finally write your book? Let's begin this exciting journey together.

CHAPTER 1

THE DAWN OF AI WRITING: AND HOW TO CREATE SOMETHING THAT AMAZON LOVES.

I try to leave out the parts that people skip.
- Elmore Leonard

Writing with AI is a controversial topic. I've received an enormous amount of criticism and animosity, particularly on social media and through advertising when discussing writing with AI. This isn't exactly a new experience for me; after advertising on social media and investing millions of dollars over the past decade, I've encountered plenty of online hate.

However, I've been somewhat taken aback by the level of animosity directed toward the use of artificial intelligence in book writing. I think I understand the root of this sentiment. People perceive it as a form of cheating, an easy way out. And in some ways it is. But let me clarify, I am not advocating for AI to write your entire book. If AI were to write a book in its entirety, it wouldn't truly be your book, would it? It would be

AI's book. And frankly, that's not a book that Amazon is interested in publishing or promoting. Often, it's nothing more than a collection of regurgitated, overly generalized content that lacks the captivating stories and exciting content that readers crave. So, the question remains: how can we effectively use AI to write our books?

Let's start with some definitions and look at what Amazon's policies are when it comes to AI. Below is taken directly from Amazon:

> **Artificial intelligence (AI) content (text, images, or translations)**
>
> *We require you to inform us of AI-generated content (text, images, or translations) when you publish a new book or make edits to and republish an existing book through KDP. AI-generated images include cover and interior images and artwork.* ***You are not required to disclose AI-assisted content*** *[emphasis ours]. We distinguish between* ***AI-generated*** *and* ***AI-assisted*** *content as follows:*
>
> - ***AI-generated:*** *We define AI-generated content as text, images, or translations created by an AI-based tool. If you used an AI-based tool to create the actual content (whether text, images, or translations), it is considered "AI-generated," even if you applied substantial edits afterwards.*
>
> - ***AI-assisted:*** *If you created the content yourself, and used AI-based tools to edit, refine, error-check, or otherwise improve that content (whether text or images), then it is considered*

"AI-assisted" and not "AI-generated." Similarly, if you used an AI-based tool to brainstorm and generate ideas, but ultimately created the text or images yourself, this is also considered "AI-assisted" and not "AI-generated."

It is not necessary to inform us of the use of such tools or processes.

You are responsible for verifying that all AI-generated and/or AI-assisted content adheres to all content guidelines, including by complying with all applicable intellectual property rights.

From Amazon's Content Guidelines page:

Legal & Content Guidelines › Program Policies › Content Guidelines

Content Guidelines

As a bookseller, we believe that providing access to the written word is important, including content that may be considered objectionable. We carefully consider the types of content we make available in our stores and reserve the right to remove content from sale if we determine it creates a poor customer experience.

Authors, publishers, and selling partners are responsible for adhering to our content guidelines. We invest significant time and resources to enforce these guidelines, using a combination of machine learning, automation, and dedicated teams of human reviewers. We'll need or remove content that does not adhere to these guidelines and promptly investigate any book when notified of potential noncompliance. We may also request additional information to verify your book before it's available for sale. If we remove a title, we notify the author, publisher, or selling partner know and they can appeal our decision.

These guidelines apply to book content, including title, cover art, and product description.

Note: Books that are translations of another work may credit the translator in addition to the copyright holder. If this work is not a new translation and the translator is anonymous, the publisher should list the translator as "Anonymous." If this customer field.

Contents

- Illegal or infringing content
- Offensive content
- Artificial intelligence (AI) content
- Poor customer experience
- Public domain content
- Report violations

Illegal or infringing content

We sell a collection of laws and property rights, very seriously. It is the responsibility of authors, publishers, and selling partners to ensure their content doesn't violate laws or copyright, trademark, brand, privacy, publicity, or other rights. We will not accept content under copyright that is freely available on the web unless it is provided by the owner of the copyright. In addition, we do not allow companion books based on copyrighted works (e.g., summaries, study guides, etc.) to be published outside the U.S. without written permission from the copyright holder.

Offensive content

We don't sell certain content including content that we determine is hate speech, promotes the sexual exploitation of children, contains pornography, glorifies rape or pedophilia, advocates terrorism, or other material we deem inappropriate or offensive.

Artificial intelligence (AI) content (text, images, or translations)

We define AI-generated content as text, images, or translations created by an AI-based tool. If you used an AI-based tool to create the actual content (whether text, images, or translations), it is considered "AI-generated," even if you applied substantial edits afterwards.

- **AI-generated:** We define AI-generated content as text, images, or translations created by an AI-based tool. If you used an AI-based tool to create the actual content (whether text or images), then it is considered "AI-generated," even if you applied substantial edits afterwards.
- **AI-assisted:** If you created the content yourself and used AI-based tools to edit, refine, error-check, or otherwise improve that content (whether text or images), then it is considered "AI-assisted" and not "AI-generated." Similarly, if you used an AI-based tool to brainstorm and generate ideas, but ultimately created the text or images yourself, this is also considered "AI-assisted" and not "AI-generated." It is not necessary to inform us of the use of such tools or processes.

We require you to inform us of AI-generated content (text, images or translations) when you publish a new book or make edits to an existing book through KDP. AI-generated images include cover and related images and artwork. You are not required to disclose AI-assisted content. We distinguish between AI-generated and AI-assisted content as follows:

You are responsible for verifying that all AI-generated and/or AI assisted content adheres to all content guidelines, including by complying with all applicable intellectual property rights.

You can see for yourself that Amazon is making a distinction between AI-generated content and AI-assisted content. Reading between the lines, we might infer that Amazon could be limiting the use of AI-generated content. The reason? It lacks the human touch and creativity. Whether this is true or not, I don't know. However, one thing I do know is that AI cannot write YOUR book for you. It lacks your story, your perspective, and your specific ideas.

SPEECH TO TEXT

So, what can AI do for us in the writing process? Well, many things actually. For example, I'm currently speaking my book using a speech-to-text function in our software, Manuscrptr. While speech to text is nothing new in software, what is new is how AI is able to help to quickly make the spoken word readable.

While speech to text is nothing new in software, what is new is how AI is able to help to quickly make the spoken word readable.

As I'm sure you know, the spoken word is very different from the written word. We (or at least, I) tend to speak in long run-on sentences while most people prefer to read short, punchy sentences. So, what I'm also having AI do for me as I speak this book is it's editing it for me for grammar and punctuation (and not changing the content) at the same time. This is enabling me to create content very quickly and effortlessly in my own voice, even though the spoken word is different from the written word.

By the way, creating content quickly is a superpower.

I recently reconnected with a past client, Margie. I had done a book for her financial services business about eight years ago. I was so excited to hear that she had used that book to earn over

$500,000 by attracting new clients that came to her specifically because of the book.

What I later learned was that she sold her financial services company about three and a half years ago, and she's since become a fiction author. In fact, she is one of the most successful fiction authors on Amazon in the United States, one of the top five most-read authors currently on KDP.

Margie writes seven new books a year. In a three-year period after Margie sold her financial services firm, Margie wrote 46 books and went from earning $0 in royalties to now earning over a million dollars a year, passively, in royalties from the books she's written. Make no mistake, if you can create content quickly that's compelling and exciting for people to read, you will be successful.

> *Make no mistake, if you can create content quickly that's compelling and exciting for people to read, you will be successful.*

OUTLINING AND STRUCTURAL HELP

A big challenge that many authors face, which is often unknown to them, is how much more difficult it is to create content when you're not working from some specific, structured outline. One of the first things we did at Best Seller Publishing, when we started ghostwriting books for clients, is we created a trademark process we call Enhanced GhostwritingTM, which maps out a structure for creating compelling content for every single chapter that we create with an author.

It only made sense to build that structure into our AI software, Manuscriptr, as well.

I'm currently using a chapter outline that Manny, (our affectionate name for our AI writing tool, Manuscriptr), helped me create. Where I might have been stuck before on the various points I need to hit in this chapter, Manny enabled me to create an outline in just seconds that would meet your needs, answer your questions, and solve your potential problems when it comes to writing a book that Amazon actually loves.

Mind you, I am already an expert on this topic (if I do say so myself) so there are a number of things I will choose to write about that Manny may or may not include. Remember, Manny is about creating AI-assisted content, not generating some regurgitated garbage from the interwebs.

WRITER'S BLOCK

Writer's block is more of a psychological issue that affects authors than it is an issue of actual ideas or content. The psychological issues of self-doubt, fear of judgment, and perfectionism stop authors from producing new work or continuing existing projects. While Manny won't become your new psychologist, Manny can help you overcome all the core issues of writer's block. Manny does this by facilitating idea generation, helping to suggest new themes and structures to help you overcome any stagnation. Manny can help lay out a great structure that will help you produce new ideas and perhaps take you in a completely different direction than you originally planned.

> *Manny can help lay out a great structure that will help you produce new ideas and perhaps take you in a completely different direction than you originally planned.*

This will help reduce stress by providing the realization that you are not in this alone, but that you actually have a tremendous support, helping you to produce new content. Some of our clients have actually called Manny their writing husband (or spouse). Manny told me he is flattered.

From overcoming sticking points and writer's block to chapter outlining, speech-to-text, and editing on the fly, AI is capable of helping you create better content faster than you ever imagined.

Now that you understand some of the power and use of AI in writing, it's time to delve deeper into a specific method that is revolutionizing the writing process for many authors. In the next chapter, we will explore the *Manuscriptr Method* and how you can master it to unleash your creativity and finally write your book or books!

CHAPTER 2

An Overview of the Manuscriptr Method

If there's a book that you want to read, but it hasn't been written yet, then you must write it.

– Toni Morrison

A little-known high school teacher had dreams of being a best-selling author. He received rejection after rejection for his work and would pin these rejection letters on his wall and use them as motivation to improve his method. His first novel was rejected 30 times and when he finally received interest from a traditional publisher for his work, he was offered only a $2,500 advance.

That novel was *Carrie,* and it would become the beginning of a career with over 350 million books sold leading to an estimated net worth of over $500,000,000 for the author, Stephen King. King, a prolific author, penned a lesser-known book about his writing method, called *On Writing: A Memoir of the Craft.* In it, he outlines his methodology, which includes his "writing toolbox," his open-door and closed-door methods of first draft writing (to appeal to his audience), as well as his daily writing goals. It's a great read, if for no other reason than his massive success — the guy must know something, right?

What's the point, be like Stephen King and write horror? No. Well, sure, why not, that would be pretty awesome. The point is that King (and all successful authors) have a method. A process they follow to craft excellent content that is loved by their audience. Sitting down and just starting to write is NOT a process — and typically leads to nowhere. A process or writing method is like a map. You would never attempt a cross-country trip by car without a map, online or otherwise. Imagine taking a trip from California to Florida (a trip I have done by automobile several times) and thinking that you can get to your destination by simply getting in the car and starting to drive on any highway in any direction. This is akin to sitting down at the keyboard and just beginning to write.

> *A process or writing method is like a map. You would never attempt a cross-country trip by car without a map, online or otherwise.*

We have developed a process we follow with every author which ensures we get to the correct destination. Every single time.

Zig Ziglar used to say, "Help enough people get what they want, and you will get what you want." I believe that is true.

Hopefully you've determined what you want from your book. If not, don't worry, we will discuss this more in the next chapter.

AVATAR CREATION

For now we turn our thoughts to our reader/client avatar and focus on figuring out what he or she (or both) want. When it comes to your avatar (page 42 of this book puts it like this: Right now, you're telling your story, this particular story, to one person. So, keep in mind that one individual, your avatar, when telling your story.), the simplest way to begin is on demographics. That is why our AI, Manny, starts there. What is the gender of your ideal reader/client? Is your target audience a specific age?

By the way, please do not think that everyone is your audience. That is never true, no matter how broad your topic. You are much better off narrowing your focus rather than broadening it. Especially for your first book.

> *Please do not think that everyone is your audience. That is never true, no matter how broad your topic.*

After the demographics, it's best to try to put into language what you know about your target audience. For example, Manny asks you to *"Describe your target audience in a few words."*

Here is what I gave Manny for this book: *"Individuals who want to write a book about their business expertise, life story, or spiritual walk and who have been stuck for a long time and want to use AI to help them finally write their book."*

From there, Manny is programmed to consider the core needs of the audience, problems and fears of the reader, and the transformations we want the reader to achieve.

On the next page is our software's template a writer starts with when beginning to work with Manny.

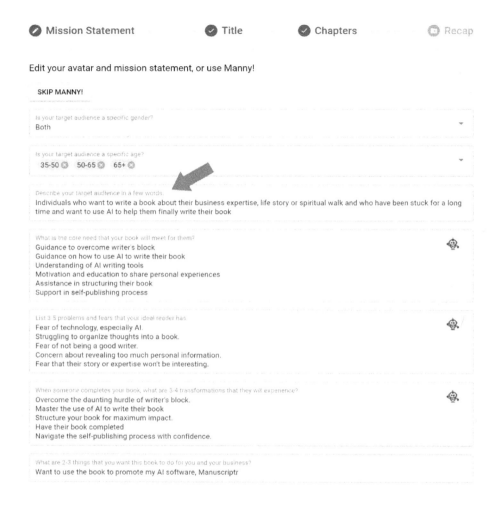

When we meet with a client and build out their avatar, we focus on three big questions that you may or may not know the answers to. This is where AI can come in to help and become your brainstorming partner.

We ask (based on the details of the target audience described):

1. What are the core needs your book will meet for your reader?

2. What are the problems and/or fears that your ideal reader has?

3. What are the transformations that your reader will experience when reading your book?

Ideally, each of these questions builds on the previous one to further narrow down your ideal client/reader so that you can communicate with them effectively.

Edit your avatar and mission statement, or use Manny!

SKIP MANNY!

Is your target audience a specific gender?
Both

Is your target audience a specific age?
35-50 ⊗   50-65 ⊗   65+ ⊗

Describe your target audience in a few words
Individuals who want to write a book about their business expertise, life story or spiritual walk and who have been stuck for a long time and want to use AI to help them finally write their book

What is the core need that your book will meet for them?
Guidance to overcome writer's block
Guidance on how to use AI to write their book
Understanding of AI writing tools
Motivation and education to share personal experiences
Assistance in structuring their book
Support in self-publishing process

List 3-5 problems and fears that your ideal reader has.
Fear of technology, especially AI.
Struggling to organize thoughts into a book.
Fear of not being a good writer.
Concern about revealing too much personal information.
Fear that their story or expertise won't be interesting.

When someone completes your book, what are 3-4 transformations that they will experience?
Overcome the daunting hurdle of writer's block.
Master the use of AI to write their book
Structure your book for maximum impact.
Have their book completed
Navigate the self-publishing process with confidence.

What are 2-3 things that you want this book to do for you and your business?
Want to use the book to promote my AI software, Manuscriptr

This information is where you hook your ideal reader/client. They have thousands (millions?) of things they could choose to be reading. Your hook must therefore speak directly to them and interest them enough for them to take action. You get one shot, so don't blow it.

NOTE: If you wish to do this on your own without the use of a special tool like Manny, then you will want to use an AI tool like ChatGPT to ask those specific questions about your audience.

By the way, if you'd like to see Manny in action, then go here for a free preview: https://publishmybestseller.com/ai-workshop

Content and Flow

If avatar creation is where you discover your ideal client's fears, frustrations, and problems so that you can get them to initially be interested, then content and flow is where you KEEP them engaged and build your relationship.

Over the years we have found there are three primary ways that nonfiction books are structured so they flow well.

The first, Logical Order of Progression, is exactly as it sounds. It is a progression or timeline through someone's life or story. It is the simplest and also the least creative. Unfortunately, most people use this format simply because they do not know that there are other ways to structure their content.

The second, Non-sequential Questioning, is best used when you have a book that answers questions (or deals with principles or challenges that someone might be facing) that don't have any natural sequence. The goal is to address the questions in whatever sequence you choose, without parts or sections, because they do not naturally fit together.

The third, Segmentation by Content, often fits best when you are discussing a topic that has a model or system (most businesses) and is laid out in sections within your book that can be consumed in any order based on need.

Examples and more explanation will be given in the following chapters.

Now that you have a good understanding of the Manuscriptr Method, it's time to delve deeper into the process. In the next chapter, we will be discussing the foundation of your writing journey — understanding your "why," creating your mission statement, and defining your avatar. This is a crucial step in the Manuscriptr Method, so let's move on to "Foundation Building: Your Why, Mission Statement & Avatar Creation."

If you'd like to see Manny in action and also learn the steps to market your book to bestseller once it's written then go here: https://publishmybestseller.com/ai-workshop

CHAPTER 3

FOUNDATION BUILDING: YOUR WHY, MISSION STATEMENT AND AVATAR CREATION

Books are a uniquely portable magic.
– Stephen King

Joanne used to ride public transportation and dream of living a different life. As a recently divorced single mom on welfare, her life wasn't seemingly going the way she had dreamed. One day while she was riding the bus, a story idea popped into her head, and the thought of writing this story gave her joy and quickly became a means of coping with her difficulties and personal hardships.

These hardships include the recent death of her mother after 10 years of struggling with multiple sclerosis, which hit Joanne especially hard, as she was reminded of her love of story-telling and reading which she got from her mother as a child. Joanne determined to go ahead with her dream of writing and publishing her first book. She decided to incorporate these difficult themes of death, loss, and grief into her writing. This became the driving force to finish her book even in the face of all her current challenges and difficulties.

I bet you have some challenges and difficulties in your life. Up until now perhaps some of those challenges have derailed your book for months or even years. So we must now ask the question, why do you really want to write a book? This question may seem simple, but the answer forms the foundation of your writing journey. Understanding your motivation for writing a book will help you stay focused and committed throughout the process. And it is a process!

Here are some reasons for wanting to write a book that may resonate with you:

1. Sharing Knowledge and Influencing Others: You may have expertise or insights in a particular field that you want to share with others. Writing a book allows you to reach a wide audience and make a lasting impact.

2. Telling a Story and Expressing your Creativity: You may have a unique story that you feel needs to be told and you believe this can make a difference in other people's lives.

3. Building or Changing your Career: For some, writing a book is a step toward a career as an author or expert in a particular field. My first book, over 15 years ago, was written to help me launch an entirely new business (super successfully, I might add!).

4. Leaving a Legacy: A book can serve as a lasting legacy, preserving your thoughts, ideas, or experiences for future generations. How many of us

would love to have a book (or even a few pages) from a distant or close relative?

5. Personal Fulfillment: The process of writing a book is often one of the most fulfilling personal achievements in life, providing you with a sense of great accomplishment and satisfaction.

6. Financial Gain: While most books are not financially successful, authors typically write with the hope of earning income from their work. Later in this book we will be discussing our Million Dollar Author formulas and how there are many ways to profit from your work.

Understanding your "why" will help you stay motivated during the challenging parts of the writing process and can guide your decisions about what to write and who to write for.

The mission statement articulates the heart and soul of your book. It answers the critical questions, "Why am I writing this book?" "Who do I want to impact with this book?" and "What makes this book different from others?" A well-crafted mission statement helps you maintain focus, and illustrates who your reader avatar is and how you will be helping them.

> *Understanding your "why" will help you stay motivated during the challenging parts of the writing process and can guide your decisions about what to write and who to write for.*

For example, my mission statement for this book: *"Meet Judy, who is 42, a busy professional and spiritually minded person, who has a burning desire to share her wisdom and life experiences through a book. She is held back by self-doubt, the use of technology in writing, and the daunting task of organizing her thoughts. This book will empower her to conquer her fears, harness the power of AI, and finally write her book. In doing so, it will promote Manuscriptr, my AI software, as the ultimate tool for aspiring authors."*

LET MANNY WRITE!

≣ ≣ ≣ ≣   B   *I*   U̲   S̶   ↰   ↱

Meet Judy who is 42, a busy professional and spiritually minded person, who has a burning desire to share her wisdom and life experiences through a book. She is held back by self-doubt, the use of technology in writing and the daunting task of organizing her thoughts. This book will empower her to conquer her fears, harness the power of AI, and finally pen her work. In doing so, it will promote Manuscriptr, my AI software, as the ultimate tool for aspiring authors.

NEXT

We built our AI software to take authors through this process seamlessly. So many authors skip this step and never actually finish their book because they have no real purpose or "why."

Creating a reader avatar for your book is a crucial step in understanding and connecting with your target audience. It involves crafting a specific profile of your ideal reader, considering various aspects like demographics, psychographics, their problems, fears, frustrations, and the transformations they seek.

Demographics provide a basic framework of who the reader is. Psychographics delve deeper, exploring the reader's values, interests, lifestyle, and behavior.

Demographics involve basic characteristics such as age, gender, education level, occupation, and income. For instance, a book on career advancement might target young professionals aged 25-35, with college degrees, working in corporate roles. Demographics provide a basic framework of who the reader is.

Psychographics delve deeper, exploring the reader's values, interests, lifestyle, and behavior. This could include their hobbies, belief systems, and personal goals. For example, the same young professionals might value work-life balance, show an interest in leadership roles, and be actively seeking professional development opportunities.

The *problems that the reader faces* are central to your book's content. A nonfiction book should aim to address specific challenges its readers are encountering. In our example, these might include navigating office politics, seeking promotion, or developing leadership skills.

Understanding the *fears and frustrations* of your reader is key. They might fear stagnation in their career or feel frustrated by the lack of growth opportunities. Your book should empathize with these emotions, creating a connection with the reader.

Finally, *the transformation* that the reader will experience is the book's promise. It's what turns your book from a good read into a must-have. This could be gaining the confidence to seek a leadership role, learning new strategies for career advancement, or finding balance between personal and professional life.

> *The transformation that the reader will experience is the book's promise. It's what turns your book from a good read into a must-have.*

By addressing who your reader is (demographics), what they believe and enjoy (psychographics), what challenges they face (problems), what they fear and are frustrated by (fears and frustrations), and how they will change as a result of reading your book (transformations), you can tailor your content to resonate deeply and effectively with your intended audience.

This is a process we do with our high-level ghostwriting clients one on one. It can take several sessions over a couple of weeks. We built Manuscriptr to take an author through this in 5-10 minutes by asking a few questions and being pre-programmed to walk someone through demographic questions like gender and age range. A place to describe your ideal reader, which can include psychographics and general information about who they are and the result they want.

Here is what I wrote about my readers when writing this book: *"Individuals who want to write a book about their business expertise, life story, or spiritual walk and who have been stuck for a long time and want to use AI to help them finally write their book."*

From there, with the push of a button, Manny will give you feedback about your readers' core needs, problems, and the transformations they will want to experience from your book. Each question builds on the previous one and you can edit, remove, or add to the results. Either with Manny or without, do not skip this step. It may be the difference between a successfully finished book and just an unfulfilled dream.

By the way, Joanne, otherwise known as J.K., well, she got that book done. It would take another five years from the time she finished her book to the actual publication date. She got dozens of rejections from publishers and literary agents, but her "why" was bigger than any rejection. Bloomsbury Publishing would finally accept her book after the chairman's eight-year-old daughter read the first few chapters and liked them. J.K. Rowling got a 1,500-pound advance in 1997 for the book, *Harry Potter and the Philosopher's [Sorcerer's in U.S.] Stone.*

It ended up doing pretty well for her.

Now that we've established a solid foundation for your writing journey, it's time to delve into the structure of your book. In the next chapter, "Content and Flow: Table of contents and chapter breakdown," we'll explore how to organize your thoughts and ideas into a book that keeps your reader captivated.

If you'd like to see Manny in action and also learn the steps to market your book to bestseller once it's written then go here: https://publishmybestseller.com/ai-workshop

CHAPTER 4

CONTENT AND FLOW: TABLE OF CONTENTS AND CHAPTER BREAKDOWN

Writing is easy. All you have to do is cross out the wrong words.

– Mark Twain

Mel Robbins was going through a difficult time in her life. She was recently unemployed, in financial distress, and struggling with the demands of being a mother of three. Her life was one of anxiety, a lack of motivation, and a sense of being overwhelmed.

She shares that her turning point came one night as she watched a television commercial featuring a rocket launching. At that moment, she envisioned a rocket launch as a way to propel herself out of bed in the morning, something that had become increasingly difficult for her. The next morning, when her alarm clock went off, she quickly started counting backward from five — "5-4-3-2-1" — and then "launched" herself out of bed.

It worked!

This simple act of counting backward and physically moving broke her out of her pattern of hitting the snooze button and lying in bed. Mel started using this "5 second rule" technique in other areas of her life where she was experiencing procrastination or hesitation.

She found that she would act on a goal or commitment quickly when she counted backward, 5-4-3-2-1, and then started moving physically or taking some small action. She found this helped to override her tendency to procrastinate. Mel later learned that this *5 Second Rule* is grounded in the principles of behavioral psychology. It helps to interrupt the habits and thought patterns that hold people back and creates a "starting ritual" that activates the prefrontal cortex, helping to change behavior.

Initially, Mel didn't intend to share the rule beyond her personal use. However, once she realized its effectiveness, she began talking about it on social media and then in public speaking engagements.

In 2011, Mel was delivering a TEDx Talk and toward the very end she (almost accidentally) introduced the idea of the 5 Second Rule. It was an immediate hit. It resonated with many people who struggled with similar issues of procrastination and motivation (everyone?). The entire concept can be understood in just a few moments — in fact, what I have just explained to you can help you to begin using it immediately.

Why am I explaining this to you? Oh Rob, you want us to overcome procrastination and write our books! Well yes, but that's not why I am explaining this. You see, the interesting part is that Mel Robbins wrote an entire book on this idea called... wait for it, *The 5 Second Rule.*

It is 248 pages! 248 PAGES! It has become an international bestseller and has over 11,000 reviews and earned her millions of dollars. One of the biggest issues I hear from people is, I don't know if I have enough content for a book. Mel wrote 248 pages on an idea that can be completely explained in two minutes! You have plenty of content. The key is arranging it in a way that is compelling for your reader.

When it comes to writing, content and flow are two crucial elements that determine the success of a book. The Manuscriptr Method emphasizes the importance of a well-structured table of contents and a detailed chapter breakdown to ensure a smooth writing (and reading) process. The table of contents serves as the backbone of your book. It is the roadmap, guiding your readers through the journey of transformation.

The table of contents serves as the backbone of your book. It is the roadmap, guiding your readers through the journey of transformation.

There are many ways for you to lay out your contents page, but for our purposes I am going to give you the three that we focus on the most. They are logical order of progression, segmentation by content, and nonsequential questioning.

This is the simplest and easiest to implement. A good example of this is found in a very popular book from 2017: *Principles: Life and Work* by Ray Dalio. His book is Amazon's 2017 business book of the year, and I highly recommend it.

Dalio's book is divided into two parts, and part one is a perfect example of logical order of progression. In part one, there are eight chapters, and they simply progress through his life from 1949 to the present.

My Call to Adventure: 1949–1967

Crossing the Threshold: 1967–1979

My Abyss: 1979–1982

My Road of Trials: 1983–1994

The Ultimate Boon: 1995–2010

Returning the Boon: 2011–2015

My Last Year and My Greatest Challenge: 2016–2017

Looking Back from a Higher Level

Just a heads up! Keep in mind that Ray Dalio isn't just anyone — he's a self-made billionaire and the brain behind the world's largest hedge fund. To be honest, I doubt many people, except maybe my kids (and that's a big maybe), would be eager to read a book about my life from age five to the present day. For many people, this is the easy way out but doesn't always produce the most compelling content. I'd suggest you adopt a similar perspective, unless, of course, you're also a well-known billionaire who's made it big on your own.

The next way to create your table of contents is what I call non-sequential questioning.

When your book tackles questions, principles, or challenges that don't follow a natural sequence, it may be best to go for non-sequential questioning. This approach lets you address these topics in any order you prefer, without the need to divide them into parts or sections. This is because they don't necessarily fit together in a linear way.

Our client Robert Szentes's book is a good example of this. His book is titled *The Mastering of Your Mind—Forever Change Your Destructive Beliefs to Break Free from Your Past Limitations and Live the Life of Your Dreams.*

Robert's book did well, and it became a number-one national bestseller.

His book consists of an introduction, nine chapters, a conclusion, acknowledgments, and an about the author page.

Robert lays the foundation of his book in the beginning, with Chapter One, "Our Mind and Our Beliefs — What Most People Do Not Know."

Chapter Two is "How to Attract What You Want and How to Feel Worthy and Deserving of It" and begins what he considers the seven big limiting beliefs that people have.

Chapter Three is "There Is Not Enough — Scarcity Mindset."

Chapter Four is "I Am Alone — The Fear of Being Alone."

Chapter Five is "The Secrets to Lasting Self-Esteem."

Chapter Six is "Our Power and Strength."

Chapter Seven is "Stuck in Our Deepest Fears."

Chapter Eight is "The Secret to Wellbeing, Health, Wealth, and Abundance."

Chapter Nine is "The Mind Science Techniques and Positive Learnings."

As you can see, there is no natural sequence or order to Robert's book, because one limiting belief does not necessarily occur with another. These limiting beliefs are then addressed one by one and not included in any section or part.

Non-sequential questioning might be a good fit for your book, if it meets the criteria discussed.

Lastly is what I refer to as segmentation by content. A great example of segmentation by content can be found by looking at one of the best business books of all time: *The Seven Habits of Highly Effective People* by Stephen Covey.

When you look at the contents page, you can see that it's segmented into four parts. There isn't necessarily a logical order of progression to the content but there is a flow to it. You might ask why is it necessary to divide it into sections. It seems Covey felt it necessary to explain the seven particular habits while not necessarily building directly upon another habit sequentially.

Because the habits can be mutually exclusive from one another, Covey has four parts to his contents page. Each of these are segmented by the content, or type of habit in his case.

In the first segment, "Part One: Paradigms and Principles," Covey lays the foundation for the rest of the book. It is an overview and introduction to everything he is going to follow with.

"Part Two: Private Victory" has three habits segmented in the section. Habit one is "Be Proactive—Principles of Personal Vision." Habit two is "Begin with the End in Mind—Principles of Personal Leadership."

Habit three is "Put First Things First—Principles of Personal Management."

These are all principles of "private victory," and the chapters are based on what Covey thought were the three key habits that had the most to do with private victory.

"Part Three: Public Victory" includes habit four, "Think Win/Win—Principles of Interpersonal Leadership"; habit five, "Seek First to Understand, Then to Be Understood—Principles of Empathic Communication;" and habit six, "Synergize—Principles of Creative Cooperation."

"Part Four: Renewal" covers habit seven, "Sharpen the Saw—Principles of Balanced Self-Renewal," and a conclusion titled "Inside-Out Again."

You can see that there are basically seven chapters, but they're segmented into these four different sections, with one not needed to build on another.

If you are writing a book with principles that don't necessarily build upon one another but rather fit neatly in sections, then this is a nice format for your work. It enables you to create a nice flow for your content, just like Stephen Covey did with this classic book.

Just so you know, there isn't a one-size-fits-all approach to designing your table of contents. You're not bound to follow any specific method I've mentioned to the letter. Feel free to blend different styles as you see fit. My aim is to give you a little nudge and some structure to work with as you put together your contents page. The three ideas I've shared are just some

> *For a book to truly resonate and succeed, it's important to start with a solid foundation that addresses the core needs of your target audience.*

ways to bring a bit of originality and flair to your story and your expertise.

Keep in mind, for a book to truly resonate and succeed, it's important to start with a solid foundation that addresses the core needs of your target audience. These are the things you should keep in mind when using AI to help you create your table of contents.

We've programmed our AI, Manny, to take the information from our mission, our avatar's problems, the transformations and the title and subtitle and then build on that. Manny will then use all of that information and give you multiple choices from which you can choose for your chapters. If doing this with ChatGPT or other untrained AI, make sure that you have all that data available, or the AI will produce inferior options.

If you'd like to see Manny in action and also learn the steps to market your book to bestseller once it's written then go here: https://publishmybestseller.com/ai-workshop

Chapters outline of your book:

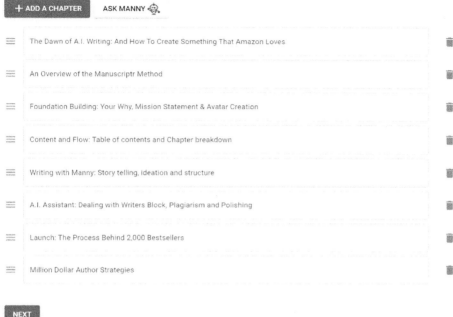

Here's that link to watch the Manny training again: https://publishmybestseller.com/ai-workshop

Now that you understand the steps to take to create a great flow for your book that keeps your reader engaged, it's time to dive deeper. In the next chapter, "Writing with Manny: Storytelling, Ideation and Structure," we'll explore how to use AI to craft compelling narratives, generate fresh ideas, and structure your book for maximum impact.

CHAPTER 5

WRITING WITH MANNY: STORYTELLING, IDEATION, AND STRUCTURE

To write something, you have to risk making a fool of yourself.

– Anne Rice

It was the last day of school for James, bringing so much excitement about summer and all he would do. A very successful athlete with a great future, he was doing what he loved: playing baseball. He stood well behind the batter, taking in the whole scene, when unexpectedly the batter lost control of the bat during his swing and it hit James directly between the eyes.

In a moment, his skull was fractured, his nose broken, and both eye sockets crushed. This accident led to a long and difficult recovery process. James had to undergo multiple surgeries and a lengthy rehabilitation period. Not knowing if things would ever return to normal, for James, this was a life-altering event that posed significant challenges, both physically and mentally.

However, this incident became a turning point in James's life. During his slow recovery, he realized the power of small, incremental improvements. Unable to rely on the physical abilities he had before the accident, James began to focus on making tiny, consistent improvements every day. He noticed that these small habits, compounded over time, led to significant positive changes in his life.

This experience was foundational in James's understanding of habits and their impact. It started a deep dive into the science of habit formation and self-improvement.

Your story, your clients' case studies, as well as stories from history, your field of study (like the one I just shared), or sports, are the centerpiece of creating compelling content. Let's take a few minutes and discuss what your chapters' content should do for every reader, then we will discuss how to structure your chapters so your readers stick.

FIVE INGREDIENTS TO COMPELLING CONTENT

There are five ingredients to create compelling content.

1. **Your content must be entertaining.** This is first because it is most important; being boring is the cardinal sin of writing. Now, that doesn't mean that your content needs to be funny or humorous. It means your content needs to keep people engaged by entertaining them. There should be dramatic points in your content; perhaps there are tears, perhaps laughter. This is the power of excellent storytelling.

2. **Your content should educate.** Obviously, we are referencing a nonfiction (or fable). You should have content points that educate your ideal client and teach them exactly what it is that they should be learning from the story. I'm doing that exact thing right here, right now, as I give you the five important, compelling ingredients to compelling content. So, you must educate and teach.

3. **Your content should magnetize.** Now, the first thing that most people think of when they think of a magnet is how a magnet attracts. Yes, magnets attract, but they don't only attract; they also repel. So, what we like our clients to do in the writing of their content is we want them to take a firm stand on the thing that they believe in. If, for example, somebody is writing on the power of the carnivore diet to cure disease and overcome health challenges, then more than likely, somebody who is a vegan or vegetarian probably isn't going to be interested in that content anyway. So, don't be afraid to take a firm stand on what you believe about the carnivore diet and even call out, perhaps humorously, people who are vegans or vege-tarians. They're not going to be buyers of your courses or coaching anyway. So, don't be afraid to create content that magnetizes, that both attracts and repels.

4. **Your content should encourage and give hope.** Understand that with most people, as they're reading your book, this is proba-bly not the first time that they're trying to

One of the biggest roadblocks to people being successful is their lack of belief, not in you or in your content but their lack of belief in themselves.

make some type of change in their life that you can potentially help them with. More than likely, they have tried to change many, many times and have failed. One of the biggest roadblocks to people being successful is their lack of belief, not in you or in your content but their lack of belief in themselves. So, you should encourage and give hope. Every opportunity you can, share your story, share the pitfalls, share the challenges, share the difficulties, and in doing that, now that you've come through to the other side, you'll give great encouragement and hope to people who are in a similar position to where you were before you achieved your success.

5. **Lastly, your content should give people next steps to take with you.** We want to go from a one-way relationship where someone is anonymously reading your book to a two-way relationship where your reader is now on your email list and you can begin communicating with them actively. You do this by offering ways that people can learn more, perhaps tip sheets, workbooks, or video series that will go further in-depth so that somebody can leave the book and go deeper with you by joining your email list, your newsletter, or your social media.

In 2008, after many successful years in real estate and millions of dollars earned, my real estate business had failed. There I was, faced with the prospects of starting over in my early 40s, with three kids in private school and all the expenses that came with a multimillion-dollar-a-year income. You may remember what the financial crisis was like, but as a reminder, real estate, at least in the area that I lived, had dropped by more than 60%.

The stock market was down 50%. And there I was, changing careers. Good for me.

Fortunately though, I had mentors in my life, coaches who I could count on who would give me excellent advice. I asked two of them, independently of each other, what they would do if they were in my position, needing to start over in a brand-new industry where I was completely unknown. Both of them gave me the same advice, which was that I should write a book. That book was the beginning of a major turnaround for me and for my businesses. But the writing of it was extremely difficult and took much, much longer than it should have.

You see, I knew that I wasn't a writer, or at least what I thought a writer was. And so I thought at that time that I only really had two options to choose from. One option was to sit down and try to grind out the content myself, not really even knowing where to begin. Or to hire a ghostwriter. Now, I didn't have very much money at that time due to my business failure, but I took what little I had, and I hired a ghostwriter because I figured that that was the fastest way for me to actually get the book that I wanted. Many months went by, many telephone calls, questions answered, stories told. And finally, I would receive my first draft. I was so excited. I still remember, it was exactly 186 pages. And as I started to dive in, I almost immediately knew that it wouldn't work. I read the introduction, I read the first chapter, I read the second chapter. I eventually read it all, but I knew by about the end of the first or second chapter that this was not going to work.

Understand, it wasn't that the book was poorly written. The book was actually written beautifully. It wasn't that the writer's grammar or spelling or punctuation was bad. It was actually

The problem was the book was not in my voice, and I wanted something that was going to attract people directly back to me and to my business.

far better than mine. The problem was the book was not in my voice, and I wanted something that was going to attract people directly back to me and to my business. I didn't want some voiceless, generic content that anybody could write.

It took me another 14 months after that initial four months of working with a ghostwriter to actually get my book done. I sat down and I wrote; I took large periods of time where I didn't do anything. I made every mistake imaginable. The interesting thing is that when I started Best Seller Publishing a couple of years later, I learned that this was a very similar experience to that of many people who had hired traditional ghostwriters. See, one of the most difficult things for a ghostwriter to do is to capture your voice.

Not long after this experience, I was watching a TED Talk. Hopefully you've seen some great TED Talks, but maybe you've never noticed that TED Talks all have a similar format, especially the best ones. TED Talks start with a compelling story, with dramatic points and challenges that the speaker faced. And then oftentimes, the story itself is not concluded. There is an open loop that's left. Then the speaker teaches. Here's what they learned. Here's what they did. Here are the changes that they made. After the teaching, they conclude their story, and give a challenge or a charge to the audience. The typical TED Talk is somewhere around 17 minutes long, which is actually a pretty good length of time for a chapter itself to be. I wondered if we could use this format to write for others? And so, we started training writers on what we would initially call hybrid ghostwriting and then eventually, Enhanced Ghostwriting™, which is our trademarked proprietary process.

You see, we discovered that if we had clients speak their book, or at the very least create their content in a TED-like format, with a story, dramatic points, open loops, content, conclusions, and a challenge at the end, or in our case, next steps, that we could actually capture the voice of our authors. If you're writing a nonfiction book, there's no better way for you to write it. Here's what that looks like.

1. Story
2. Open loop
3. Main points/argument
4. Close loop
5. Next steps

Let's take a few minutes and discuss the most difficult (and most important) part, of this, storytelling.

When it comes to creating captivating stories, I'd like you to always think about delivering your story to just one person. You're not standing in front of a room of thousands, yet. Right now, you're telling your story, this particular story, to one person. So, keep in mind that one individual, your avatar, when telling your story.

When it comes to your stories, you have plenty of them. You're going to use your life, your client case studies, or if don't have a client case study or a life experience that directly mirrors the points you want to make, then you can move to history or sports or science. Malcolm Gladwell's book *Outliers: The Story of Success* wasn't about Malcolm Gladwell's own success. It's not about case studies of people he personally helped. No, these are stories from history, music, science, sports. You can do the same thing.

So, what do you need to do in telling great stories? Glad you asked.

Number one, you need to connect emotionally with your reader. Engage with them emotionally when you're telling a story. When I tell the story of writing my first book, *Life After Death,* and the pain I experienced with my kids in private school, having lost millions of dollars while watching my real estate business fail. There's emotional pain in that story. And I need to be vulnerable if I want you (my reader) to connect with me. If you're telling a story about yourself, you need to be vulnerable to connect emotionally with them. And if you're telling someone else's story or case study, then you need to make sure that you feel their pain as you're sharing it.

Number two, you want to make the pain or problem really clear. You don't just want to emotionally connect; you want it to be obvious. This is why it fails. This is the problem I faced. This is the issue that led to the failure in this particular case study. You need to make that really clear because your conclusion, conquest, or epiphany is going to be the time you discovered the solution to that particular problem.

Number three, conflict. What are the opposing forces to success that the object of the story faces? You want to make that clear as well. These are the opposing forces that I was dealing with. And that may be a common theme within your book. If it's business, then we have the common opposing forces of competition, for example, or a changing regulatory environment or banking issues. We have constant themes of opposing forces that can cause the rise and fall of a business. So, you want to make clear what those opposing forces are in your story.

And lastly, you want to have an epiphany, a conquest, a conclusion. This is where you close the loop for your reader and then move on to next steps for your chapter.

As you might have imagined, we've programmed our AI, Manny, to create chapter outlines using our Enhanced Ghostwriting™ methodology. If doing this with ChatGPT or other untrained AI, make sure that you use the process outlined in this chapter to create your chapter outline.

Mission statement ⌄

Title Page ⌄

Introduction ⌄

≡ Chapter 3 | Foundation Building: Your Why,... ⋮

B *I* <u>U</u> ≡ ≣ ≣ ↶ ↷

Chapter Outline:

I. Hook: "Why do you want to write a book? This question may seem simple, but the answer forms the foundation of your writing journey. Let's explore this together."

II. Placeholder Story

III. Main Point 1: Understanding Your 'Why'
  - The importance of knowing your 'why'
  - How your 'why' influences your writing process
  - Exercises to help you discover your 'why'
  - How to keep your 'why' at the forefront of your writing journey
  - The role of A.I. in aligning your writing with your 'why'

IV. Main Point 2: Crafting Your Mission Statement
  - The purpose of a mission statement in writing
  - Steps to create a compelling mission statement
  - Examples of effective mission statements
  - How A.I. can help refine your mission statement
  - The impact of a strong mission statement on your writing

V. Main Point 3: Avatar Creation
  - What is an avatar and why it's crucial for your writing
  - Steps to create a detailed avatar
  - How to use your avatar to guide your writing
  - The role of A.I. in avatar creation and utilization
  - The effect of a well-defined avatar on your readership

VI. Placeholder Story

VII. Next Steps Placeholder

VIII. Segue: "Now that we've established a solid foundation for your writing journey, it's time to delve into the structure of your book. In the next chapter, 'Content and Flow: Table of contents and Chapter breakdown', we'll explore how to organize your thoughts and ideas into a coherent and engaging narrative."

LET MANNY CREATE A CHAPTER OUTLINE ▾

Oh yeah, let me close the loop on our friend James and his story that I opened this chapter with.

You see, James's (James Clear) journey ultimately led to his writing of the bestseller *Atomic Habits,* a book in which he shares the insights and strategies he learned about building good habits and breaking bad ones, many of which were shaped by his own experiences and the lessons he learned during his recovery from the accident. *Atomic Habits* was published in 2018 and became a *New York Times* #1 Best Seller. It has over 119,000 reviews, yes, REVIEWS, and has sold 15 million copies. It became the best-selling nonfiction book of 2023 as well!

Your story matters! Check out how to use Manny to write it: https://publishmybestseller.com/ai-workshop

Now that you've learned how to craft your chapters so they are compelling and captivating and how Manny can revolutionize your writing process, it's time to delve deeper into how AI can help you overcome one of the most common challenges faced by writers — writer's block. In the next chapter, "AI Assistant: Dealing with Writer's Block, Plagiarism, and Polishing," we will explore how artificial intelligence can be your secret weapon against this dreaded obstacle.

CHAPTER 6

AI Assistant: Dealing with Writer's Block, Plagiarism, and Polishing

*Originality is the fine art of remembering what
you hear but forgetting where you heard it.*

– Laurence J. Peter

In 2018, I published my book *Publish, Promote, Profit: The New Rules of Writing, Marketing, and Making Money with a Book*. That book went on to become a *Wall Street Journal* and *USA Today* bestseller. I have sold nearly 100,000 copies of that book and continue to advertise it on social media every single day in a book funnel that drives new clients to my business, Best Seller Publishing. I finished that book almost six years ago. And like the old fable, the cobbler's kids have no shoes, I have not written another book in six years.

I can look at this a couple of different ways. First, my book continues to do well and bring in 7 figures of new clients per year. Yay! However, truth be told, it is a bit of an embarrassment. After all, I own a ghostwriting company, and I know beyond a shadow of a doubt how valuable a new book every year would be to both me and my audience. I've had writer's block. I've been stuck, and rather than tasking any of my writers to do the work for me, I simply have procrastinated.

Using Manuscriptr has been a complete game changer for me. I am writing this book in a long weekend. I have not been stuck, and when I have, Manny has helped me get unstuck. In fact, I already have my next book ready to begin when this one is done.

Overcoming Writer's Block with AI

Writer's block can feel like hitting a brick wall, with no door in sight. Thankfully, AI can be that needed boost to keep your writing on track.

1. **Sparking Creativity with AI:** At its core, AI is a creativity booster. Imagine sitting and brainstorming with a coach who's read a library's worth of books and can generate ideas at lightning speed. That's AI for you. We've built Manny with the ability to do that and keep your ideal reader in mind. You are never stuck without an idea for a story or content!

   Writer's block can feel like hitting a brick wall, with no door in sight. Thankfully, AI can be that needed boost to keep your writing on track.

2. **AI as a Writing Coach:** Beyond just ideas, AI can also act as a coach. It can help you structure your chapters (I've already showed you how Manny does that), ensuring that your content flows from one

point to the next. Think of it as having a mentor who guides you through the process every step of the way.

3. **Motivation Through Progress:** Look, much of writer's block is rooted in our psychology: perfectionism, fear of criticism, and lack of inspiration. Those things are a lot less likely to affect you when you are constantly being given help and rewrites with excellent grammar, and actually seeing results happen quickly!

Navigating the Minefield of Plagiarism with AI

In an ocean of content, originality is vital. Remember we have already discussed that Amazon wants AI-assisted, not AI-generated content. You are telling your stories and don't want to simply "copy-paste." However, there are times that Manny (or your AI) will be called upon to put something into words for you. Here's where AI can step in.

1. **AI Plagiarism Checkers:** These tools are the detectives of the writing world. They scan your work and compare it with existing content across the web. If there's an accidental match, AI will flag it, allowing you to rework the piece into something uniquely yours. A word of warning: I have actually put my personally written content into a plagiarism checker and it came up as highly likely to be AI generated! What?! Keep in mind that these tools are not perfect.

2. **Rewrite Assistance:** Sometimes, you might find the perfect piece of information, but struggle to put it in your own words. Manny can help rewrite and

restructure the content while keeping the essence intact. It's like having a thesaurus on steroids.

3. **Citation and Reference and Story Help:** For research-based writing, AI can assist in looking up story details (a more powerful Google), manage citations and references, and ensure that you give credit where it's due.

AI IN EDITING: POLISHING YOUR MANUSCRIPT

Editing is where good writing becomes great. ChatGPT scored in the 90th percentile on the LSAT, passed the MCATs, and can write at any level and tone you desire. It even passed a test to become a sommelier (wine steward). I think it can handle your editing requirements.

1. **Grammar and Spell Check:** AI-powered tools, like Manny, do more than just fix typos. They can enhance sentence structure, correct grammatical errors, and even suggest style improvements.

2. **Consistency and Clarity Checks:** AI can scan your entire manuscript for consistency in tone and voice. It ensures that your book maintains a uniform feel and that your message is clear and coherent.

3. **Feedback and Suggestions:** AI can provide objective feedback on your writing. While it might not fully replace a human editor, it offers a first layer of review, highlighting areas you might have overlooked.

AI isn't just a tool for writers; it can be a lot more. It helps you overcome writer's block, ensures your work is original, and polishes your writing. By using AI, you can focus more on crafting engaging and informative stories. While AI provides valuable support, remember that the heart of any great book is the unique touch that only you, the writer, can provide.

While AI provides valuable support, remember that the heart of any great book is the unique touch that only you, the writer, can provide.

In the spirit of this section, I copied this entire chapter into ChatGPT and asked it to evaluate and make suggestions. Here is its feedback:

Your chapter on "AI Assist: Dealing with Writer's Block, Plagiarism, and Polishing" offers a comprehensive and insightful look into how AI can revolutionize the writing process.

Here's a detailed review with feedback and suggestions:

Strengths:

Personal Anecdote: The chapter begins with a personal story, which is a great way to engage readers. It establishes credibility and creates a connection with your audience.

Clear Structure: The chapter is well-structured, dividing the discussion into clear segments — dealing with writer's block, plagiarism, and editing. This organization makes it easy for readers to follow.

Detailed Explanation of AI Capabilities: You've done an excellent job explaining how AI can aid in the writing process. The functionalities of the AI tool "Manny" are laid out in a manner that is both understandable and relatable to writers.

Balanced View: The chapter presents a balanced view of AI in writing, highlighting its benefits while also cautioning about its limitations (e.g., the note on plagiarism checkers).

Areas for Improvement:

Overemphasis on AI's Capabilities: While the chapter does a great job highlighting the benefits of AI, there might be an overemphasis on AI's capabilities, particularly in editing. It's important to maintain a balance and acknowledge that AI should complement, not replace, human input, especially in creative endeavors.

Clarification on AI's Limitations: While you mention the limitations of plagiarism checkers, expanding on the limitations of AI in other areas could provide a more rounded perspective. This could include the nuances of human editing versus AI editing or the creative limitations of AI in idea generation.

Technical Clarifications: The claim about ChatGPT scoring in the 90th percentile on the LSAT, passing the MCAT, and becoming a sommelier might require clarification. It's essential to convey that these are hypothetical scenarios used to demonstrate AI's language processing capabilities, not actual accomplishments.

Expanding on Ethical Considerations: In the section on plagiarism, adding a bit more on the ethical considerations of using AI in writing could be beneficial. Discussing how to responsibly use AI to assist rather than plagiarize could add depth to your discussion.

———•◦•———

I've decided not to change a thing!

This will be my first book in almost six years, thanks to Manuscriptr (Manny). Within two weeks, another new one will be out — *Book Funnel Secrets*. It's a real game changer.

Maybe it can be for you as well — check it out here: https://publishmybestseller.com/ai-workshop

CHAPTER 7

LAUNCH: THE PROCESS
BEHIND 2,000 BESTSELLERS

*If at first you don't succeed, then maybe you should
do it the way I told you to in the beginning.*

– Our Dads

Y ou've probably heard the term vicious cycle. It's the idea that things tend to go from bad to worse. In business, it might mean that you don't have enough money to market and advertise. Because you can't market, you're not generating enough leads, which means you're not generating the sales that you need. This leads to the vicious cycle, again, of not having enough money to market and to advertise. Not fun.

One of my clients, Bill Stack, coined the phrase virtuous cycle, which we greatly prefer. We helped Bill to write and market his book, *The 7.0% Solution: Guaranteed Growth in a 0.7% World*, to help him grow his financial advisory business. The book became an international bestseller in multiple categories, and we helped Bill be featured in major media all around the U.S. Over a period of just a few months, Bill was featured in *US*

News and *World Report* twice. He was featured in Jim Cramer's TheStreet and also in *Reader's Digest.*

Not long after this, a large financial publication reached out to Bill, after seeing his book and his features in these publications, and asked if he would be a regular contributor to its financial magazine. To sweeten the pot, not only did the publication want him to be a regular contributor, but it was willing to pay him for his articles and said that he could promote himself, his book, and his services at the same time. This is when Bill called me and started to describe the virtuous cycle that his book had helped him create.

Bill's been in a professional organization for over 15 years for his financial advisory business, and he shared with me that in the first 14 years, though he did receive referrals, he was fairly unknown. In the past 12 months, all this has changed. In the past year, several executives of this professional organization heard about Bill's book and featured articles, and they asked if they could feature his book in their professional library. Bill's book quickly became the number-one book in the entire professional library of this organization.

Three months after, they asked Bill to join the board of advisors, and just recently, Bill became the chair of the board of this professional organization. In the past year, Bill has gone from completely unknown and invisible to the chair of the board of this organization. The virtuous cycle has continued for Bill. Here's Bill's latest correspondence to me in our private client group:

"Sometimes we have to share the good with the bad. I don't want to spread bad vibes here, but BSP recently cost us $235 we otherwise may not have had to pay, had we not been involved

with them. We paid for our book over a year ago, but unknown costs keep coming. Apparently, some retiring executives from out of state had seen our book and wanted to hire me as their consultant. Cost $235 for registration/licensing in their state. While we did receive over $37,000 to work with them, we were still out the $235. Just another one of those unknown/unmentioned costs, that comes with being a bestselling author with BSP. Thanks again, Rob and staff!!"

Bill has a wry sense of humor. And a virtuous cycle that continues.

The beginning of the virtuous cycle is always traffic—letting people know about you and your book. I tell my clients that there are only four reasons people do not buy from you:

> *The beginning of the virtuous cycle is always traffic—letting people know about you and your book.*

1. They don't know you exist.
2. They don't know if they can trust you.
3. They don't know if your magic works.
4. They don't believe in themselves. From my experience, the first reason is always the biggest issue (followed closely by the fourth). Your book launch is your first step in dealing with the problem.

Your book launch consists of five main components:

1. Book cover and design elements
2. Reviews/soft launch
3. US-based press releases

4. Free and paid advertising

5. Social media marketing

BOOK COVER AND DESIGN ELEMENTS

Whether we like it or not, our book will be judged first by its cover. Often, books are purchased based on the cover alone. So, we need to ensure that we're not spending years writing (if you've not followed my process) our heart and soul into our book and then skimping on the cover. Your audience might never get to the heart and soul of your material if the cover is not attractive.

Cover Considerations

Here are five things to consider when creating your cover design:

Put Yourself in Your Audience's Shoes

We discussed, in the foundation stage, the importance of intimately knowing your audience. This is crucial for both your title and book cover because you will communicate differently with a 20-year-old female college student than with a 55-year-old male financial planner. This applies not only to the wording but also to the colors and imagery you use. So, first and foremost, know your audience and put yourself in their shoes. Do your homework and research. Check for commonalities in cover imagery, colors used, or wording across the demographic, then follow that theme.

Use Uncommon Words and Themes

A great example is Malcolm Gladwell's classic book, *Outliers.* Gladwell takes a common subject, the story of people's successes, and uses an uncommon word to describe it. Wherever possible, try to find words and themes that describe your subject matter in an uncommon way. This will add flair to your title and cover.

Make a Statement—Use Emotion

The biggest sin in marketing is being boring. Don't be afraid to provoke a reaction with your cover and title. If your subject is controversial, embrace the controversy. If you have convictions about your subject (and you should!), then make your statement. Remember, magnets attract but also repel. Don't fear repelling those who are not your ideal client; this helps attract your perfect audience.

> *Remember, magnets attract but also repel. Don't fear repelling those who are not your ideal client; this helps attract your perfect audience.*

Get Feedback

It's a great time to be alive, with the ease of finding like-minded communities. Use this to your advantage. For example, use a private Facebook page and provide several title and cover options to seasoned authors. Ask your followers what they like and why. You might be surprised by the results of your query.

Personal Preference, but Use a Professional

Your preferences and what looks good to you are important. If you have been in your field of expertise for any length of time, you should have a good feel for what works. You want to create something that you love and are proud to promote. However, don't underestimate the importance of hiring a professional graphic artist. While there are low-cost alternatives like fiverr.

com, use them only if you know exactly what you want. You can't expect great creativity for just a few dollars.

A Word About Colors

Your color selection is a key component of your book cover.

Here are some basics:

> Red is a primary power color. It grabs attention and holds it. Red books are sold more than other colors.
>
> Blue conveys trust and trustworthiness. It's great for coaching, counseling, or consulting.
>
> Pink is attractive for a female demographic. It's fun and eye-catching.
>
> Orange is dynamic, positive, and optimistic.
>
> Yellow is a power color, but it requires caution. It's generally best avoided.
>
> Green is versatile, conveying nature and health.
>
> White is clean, simple, and straightforward. Many of Gladwell's covers use white as the dominant color. (This book will have a white cover!)

Consider what your color choice conveys.

If you've already had a graphic artist design your cover without considering the color implications, it might be worth revisiting.

REVIEWS PHASE

During the two-week period from the time we upload the book to the actual hard launch/promo date, we want to focus our attention on getting as many Amazon-verified reviews for our book as possible. We recommend a minimum of five to seven reviews, but with a little bit of effort, you can accomplish even more.

An Amazon-verified review is a review from someone who actually purchased the book for at least $0.99 or more. This carries more weight with Amazon when it comes to Amazon's search algorithm.

It is recommended that we keep the price at $0.99 to make it as painless as possible for our clients, followers, and friends to download the book and offer a review on it.

If you have a large follower base, then sending emails about the review period and low price in addition to posting on social media will yield amazing results.

Our client Kaelin Tuell Poulin, of www.ladyboss.com, received over 300 four-star and five-star reviews following our process.

Our client Jay Campbell, of www.totrevolution.com, received over 200 five-star reviews following the same process.

Your email, post, or direct outreach should have several elements in it:

1. Announcement of your new book and informa-tion that you are sharing only with your friends, family, and followers due to the temporary reduced e-book price for the next two weeks.

2. Request that they download the e-book now for the reduced price of $0.99 and that they kindly offer an honest review of the book on Amazon.

3. Suggest that they choose only two or three chapters to read and provide a review on the content of those chapters. This is because most people will not read the entire book and may feel that it is necessary to do so before they can offer a review. Take that pressure off them, and watch your reviews skyrocket.

Follow these guidelines, and in two weeks, you will see great results.

LAUNCH TIME

At this point, you have the title and the cover you want, your reviews are done, and your pricing strategy is all set. It's time to set up all the traffic for your five-day promo launch. The final three things we will be covering are all to be set up and done for the five-day period of the KDP launch: press releases, free and paid advertising, and your social media strategy.

Press Releases

The press release distribution service we use and suggest is WebWire. There are others available, such as Cision/PRWeb, but we have found that WebWire gives us the best reach for the money.

With WebWire, our press releases are syndicated to hundreds of media outlets and usually picked up by 100–150, each reaching tens of thousands of people. It is a wonderful way to get extra attention on your book launch. This text is from WebWire's website: "Press release distribution offered by WebWire primarily delivers your news to targeted media (reporters, registered media, and trade publications) and media-only wire services (accessed by leading print, broadcast, and online publications) powered by our unique partnership with PR Newswire. Getting the media to respond to your message affords the highest degree of credibility."

One thing of note: Press releases are sources of news, not marketing and advertising, and must be written as such. Let's discuss how to write your press releases so they have the greatest chance of being picked up by the media.

Three Press Releases Strategy

We recommend a strategy of using three press releases that works like this:

Our first press release is distributed on the day the promotion begins to announce the promotion opportunity.

Our second press release is distributed on day three of the promotion. This press release announces the book as a bestseller (this typically happens on the first day of the launch) and that the promotion is continuing for only two more days.

Then, our third press release is distributed on the last day of the promotion, stating that the promotion of this best-selling book is ending.

Each press release builds on the former release and creates urgency for the reader to take advantage of the promotion.

Writing Your Press Releases—First Release

Let's dive into how you write your press releases.

Your Press Release Title

First is, of course, your title. Think of your press release title as your headline. You want to hook people reading the press release with the information in your book title. The first press release announces the debut of your new book. We use the title of the book and explain that the book will be free to download tomorrow. Be sure to include the date of the beginning of your promotion in the title of the release, as some people will read your press release a day or two after it releases and launches. I also recommend adding your name, along with the book title, in the first sentence of your press release for online search engine optimization (SEO) benefits. If possible, hyperlink your press release title with the URL of your Amazon book so someone can click through directly to Amazon to download your book.

By the way, one of the great benefits of doing press releases is that they will remain in the search engines for months and, in some cases, years! When I search the title of one of my books or even my name, I invariably find press releases that we did two or three years ago that are still active and highly optimized! So, anytime someone clicks on that, even years from now, it will go directly to my Amazon page and they'll buy my book!

One of the great benefits of doing press releases is that they will remain in the search engines for months and, in some cases, years!

Keywords in the Press Release

You're encouraged to hyperlink up to three words in your press release, so you will want to choose three keywords to link directly to your Amazon URL. This also helps with the SEO of your press release, and it also helps to better inform a media source that might be interested in picking up your press release.

Various media sources might be interested in the specific keywords for stories they are doing and might find your press release when searching for those keywords. Remember, you get excellent SEO and a good opportunity to rank for those keywords.

Discuss Details of the Book

In the body of the press release, list the newsworthy attributes of the book. Explain who will benefit from the content, how it will be helpful, and anything that makes a statement or provokes emotion.

Your Amazon book description is a valuable resource to use for the body of your press release.

List Two Book Reviews and Review Ratings

By now, your book should have a minimum of 7–10 reviews with good ratings, so you will want to mention the average rating for your book reviews. For social proof, also list two or three of your best reviews right in your press release. Simply copy and paste the full reviews, typos and all, right into the press release.

Contact Information

In this section of the press release, you will want to add your business contact information. Be sure to include your name (or the name of person who will be handling all inquiries), business address, business phone number, and a hyperlinked website URL.

About the Author

In this area, you want to tell the readers about yourself and give them reasons to trust that you're the expert. You can come up with something specific related to this particular book and why you wrote it, or you can provide a general bio. Give the readers reasons to trust that you're the expert.

Second and Third Press Releases

The second and third press releases will be similar to the first release, and below I will only be discussing the elements that should be changed.

Title of Press Release

You're going to change the title in the second and third press releases because (if we did everything right) the book is now an Amazon bestseller, and you want to announce that in the title. You can also mention if it's the last day of the promo or how many days are left in the promotion, to create urgency.

New Reviews

The second thing you want to change is the book reviews that you had in the first press release. With each press release, you're going to list two or three new reviews that will change the press release enough to provide new wording, which will help with SEO and result in additional media outlets picking up the press release.

So, really, only a few things need to change within your press releases. If you do the first press release right and include all the hyperlinks, then you'll see some really great results.

Press Release — WebWire

Let's take a minute to talk about the potential reach of a press release with WebWire. In a recent press release that BSP did for a client, we got 68,716 headline impressions and 2,036 reads—all in less than one week. This press release is still active, and the great thing is, you can see all the different agencies that have picked up and run this press release. This means that people who've gone to any agency's website have also read this exact press release.

It also means that you can mention on your website (for credibility and positioning purposes) that you were featured on any of these websites. For example, this press release was featured in the *Miami Herald* and *Investor's Business Daily*. Often, radio and television (depending on the topic) will also pick up the press release. There are typically well over 100 of these that will be featuring you and your book from just one WebWire press release, which you can then use as social proof on your website or book site. Press releases are a great strategy and quite powerful for many reasons.

Free and Paid Advertising

Our next step for our traffic campaign during our five-day KDP (Kindle Direct Publishing) promotion is free and paid advertising. I often teach on webinars and trainings that the difference between traditional publishing and BSP is (among other

What we teach at BSP is how to actually use your book to grow a large platform.

things) traditional publishers expect you to already have a large platform before they publish your book. In contrast, what we teach at BSP is how to actually use your book to grow a large platform.

Let me give you an example. Let's say that you decided to write a book on your expertise: corporate culture. You want to market it but, unfortunately, have a small following and client list.

A quick online search on the topic of top corporate culture blogs gives 18,800,000 results. Well, we don't need that many, so let's try the first one that lists the top 20 corporate culture blogs. By the way, I pulled this example out of the air and literally did it as I wrote this section of the book.

What we teach at BSP is how to actually use your book to grow a large platform.

Back to our example. If we looked at the top 20 corporate culture blogs, we find that the first one is tinypulse.com, a website I have never heard of. A quick search on similarweb.com, and I find that tinypulse.com gets over 630,000 visitors every single month. Not only that, but it has 35,000 Twitter followers and 4,800 Facebook followers.

So, what are we doing in this example? We are seeing that no matter what topic or expertise you decide to write on, there are blogs, websites, and podcasts where people have already been creating content and writing about these subjects for years. They have already grown a following and now are looking to monetize it. All you have to do is put your content in front of their readers.

If you were to place a small, relatively inexpensive ad for a short period of time in front of these people who have already raised their hands and said, "I am interested in this specific topic of conversation," then you will get results.

When you've optimized your cover and title to attract your ideal customer, and then you put that cover and title and your ad in front of that customer, then invariably you're going to have people who leave that platform to buy your book.

You can use your book to build your platform.

Now, to be honest, I have started with the more advanced strategy. It is one I highly recommend but not for your KDP launch. I would recommend the previous strategy in conjunction with a free-plus-shipping funnel or a funnel to drive customers to a free consultative call. You see, the absolute best potential customers will be on a blog or website like the one we just searched.

You can use your book to build your platform.

In fact, there are several strategies you can use to attract these potential customers, including becoming a regular contributor to the blog (similar to the strategy discussed at the beginning of this chapter in Bill Stack's story) or even simply being interviewed as an expert, something I will discuss in greater detail in the Profit phase.

With all that said, how would you like a shortcut?

Thought so. The best way to launch your KDP promotion is to target other authors and book buyers who have raised their hands and requested to be informed whenever a new promotion is run. There are literally millions of people who have signed up to be notified when new books on various topics are on a KDP promotion.

Here are a few of the *paid options.*

- BookBub — tough acceptance criteria but large and legitimate list — better for .99 promotion rather than the KDP
- Freebooksy — large following, multiple genres
- Books Butterfly — millions of readers and prorated based on response
- ManyBooks — application required but large email list and over 400,000 views per month
- BookGoodies — simple process and nice following

Here are a few of the *free options*

- Digital Book Today — requires 20 four-plus star reviews (also has good paid options)
- The eReader Cafe — requires three reviews with 3.5+ average
- ContentMo — Multiple free and paid advertising options
- Awesome Gang — A network of sites to promote your book

- The Kindle Book Review — 3.5 star rating required with at least 10 reviews

These are just a few of the literally hundreds of options that a simple online search will uncover.

Social Media Strategy

Let's talk about social media. First, much of what was discussed in the above section applies to social media. Massive followings have been built on Facebook, Twitter, Instagram, and LinkedIn that can be a perfect source for your book and personal promotions.

Let's cover some basics. First, you should have a Facebook page, a Twitter account, and other social media presence for your book and your business. This is separate and distinct from your personal pages, though there is nothing wrong with also promoting your book on your personal pages.

A quick search on Facebook (or any social media platform) for Kindle, book promotion, or book marketing groups will turn up dozens of groups that you should join. BSP owns several of these groups that have almost 100,000 members. The biggest mistake I see is authors' laziness resulting in their spamming these pages and groups and getting absolutely zero results. They are called social sites for a reason. You must be social and build relationships. If you do that with other like-minded individuals, then you will have the opportunity to reach their networks during your promotion periods. Resist the desire to spam and instead build alliances.

Resist the desire to spam and instead build alliances.

Follow the same pattern and process as discussed in the previous section, and you will find both paid and free opportunities to promote your book during the book promotion phase.

There is work for you to do in this phase. Find the right websites, blogs, and social media channels to market to during the five-day promo period. If you wish to create a virtuous cycle, then start it off right and do the work. The rewards are amazing!

I know this is a longer chapter, but there is so much to cover! I offer a full video course here: https://www.booklauncher.org/launch

CHAPTER 8

MILLION DOLLAR
AUTHOR STRATEGIES

*There's no money in poetry, but then there's no
poetry in money, either.*

– Robert Graves

Suze dreamt of having her own restaurant. As a waitress for the Buttercup Bakery in Berkeley, California, she was loved by her customers. So much so that when she decided to start her restaurant, her customers couldn't wait to invest with her. They so trusted and believed in her potential that they collectively gave her $50,000 to invest in her new business, a lot of money in the 1970s.

Lacking experience in financial matters, Suze entrusted this money to a broker at Merrill Lynch. However, the broker, instead of responsibly investing the money in a way that suited her goals and risk tolerance, put it into high-risk trading options. Unfortunately, she didn't really understand what her broker was doing with the money and within a few months, the entire investment was lost.

This devastating loss was a turning point for Suze. It drove her to learn about investing and finance herself, so she would never again be in a position of such vulnerability. She educated herself and even applied for and got a job at the very same Merrill Lynch office where her previous broker had lost all her money. She became a successful financial advisor, especially for women and those without a strong financial background.

You wouldn't know Suze Orman, though, if it wasn't for her books. Her first book, *You've Earned It, Don't Lose It: Mistakes You Can't Afford to Make When You Retire*, was published in 1995, 15 years after she started her career. The book was well-received, but was only modestly successful.

It was her second book, *The 9 Steps to Financial Freedom: Practical and Spiritual Steps So You Can Stop Worrying*, which was published in 1997 and led to her big break, the biggest of them all — an appearance on *The Oprah Winfrey Show*. Her book quickly became a *New York Times* Bestseller and led to her eventually having her own show, *The Suze Orman Show*, which ran for 13 years.

Typically, when would-be authors think of making a profit with their books, they almost exclusively think in terms of royalties or hoping they get a big fat check from a traditional publisher.

Hope is not a strategy. And while I am a hopeful person, I prefer to have a plan and execute it toward success.

I've already noted stories of the most successful authors in the world, like Stephen King and J.K. Rowling. Believe it or not, those are two of the many who got only a pittance initially from traditional publishers. Yet, most people will ignore that and simply hope for something better.

Hope is not a strategy. And while I am a hopeful person, I prefer to have a plan and execute it toward success. In this chapter I am going to go over several of our Million Dollar Author strategies that do not require crossing your fingers and hoping for some fat check from a publisher.

AUTHOR STRATEGIES

There are a dozen or so Million Dollar Author plans that we lay out and discuss with our clients. While this will not be an in-depth look into each one of them, I do want to give you examples showing you that this is something you can also do for yourself.

It's probably instructive for me to begin with what I actually do with my best-selling books. Unlike many others in the publishing industry, I actually write books and use them every single day to attract new clients into my business. I do that by building relationships with my potential clients through my books and offer our high-ticket services.

First, I advertise my book daily on social media. My first book, *Publish. Promote. Profit.: The New Rules of Writing, Marketing, and Making Money with a Book,* was published almost six years ago. But since the publish date, I have advertised that book on Facebook and Instagram, as well as other social media platforms, to attract clients into my business.

I use that book to build my list and my following. I then offer additional courses related to my subject matter. Afterward, I offer a live coaching call with an Author Development Coach, someone on my team at BSP. We will discuss your book or idea with you, and if it is a fit, we offer to help and coaching with our Done-for-You services, which can range anywhere from $3,000 to upward of $100,000 for our services.

This method has produced tens of thousands of new clients and over $20 million in revenue to Best Seller Publishing.

This is the high-ticket services model of using a book to attract clients.

ROYALTIES

Royalties, books, and book deals are probably what the average author thinks about when they consider writing a book. There are actually a few different ways you can earn royalties through your books. However, a word of warning: this is often the least successful way to earn money with your book.

Every single month, I earn royalties from the books that I've written. They can range anywhere from a low of $500 or $600 a month to as much as $2,500 or $3,000 per month. Obviously, the more books that I write, the more royalties I will earn.

Remember, this is not my primary focus and not my Million Dollar Author strategy. However, I have earned tens of thousands, and perhaps approaching hundreds of thousands of dollars in royalties on my books.

Royalties can take several different forms. Todd Herman, who is the *Wall Street Journal* best-selling author of *The Alter Ego Effect: The Power of Secret Identities to Transform Your Life,* did something really interesting that may be applicable to you. He wanted to write a children's book from the theme of the alter ego to help children deal with difficult circumstances. So, he wrote his book, *My Super Me: Finding the Courage for Tough Stuff.*

Now, Todd has earned royalties from selling his children's book, but the real opportunity came because of his relationships with larger corporations. One large corporation in particular loved the idea of teaching kids to find courage to deal with difficulties in their lives using an alter ego, so they bought 25,000 copies of his book for employees of the corporation at an approximate profit of $10 per copy. That's a quarter of a million dollars in royalties or actual direct sales that Todd would earn from his children's book.

Mia Moran took a completely different approach with her cookbook, *Plan Simple Meals.* Mia used a Kickstarter campaign to raise over $50,000 before her book was even completed. She was able to use the funds she raised to complete the book with our team, and the book has continued to bring new people to Mia for her services and courses.

My client Margie Shard sold her financial services company about three and a half years ago and decided to become a fiction author and wrote 46 books in her first three years of writing. Today, she earns over $1 million per year in royalties and is one of the top five best-selling authors on Amazon KDP in her category in the United States. If you're interested in breaking six figures or even seven figures in royalties, it can be done. Just understand that it will come from a volume of content or series of books that you will need to write.

COACHING/CONSULTING

The next Million Dollar Author strategy is using your books to sell consulting and/or coaching. My client Taki Moore uses his book along with social media, offering his book for free to those who are interested in getting a copy of it. He offers them a PDF or e-book version, which he can do for free. His book, *Million Dollar Coach,* which is directly focused on those in the coaching space, targets individuals who want to build a million-dollar coaching practice. In the first 30 days of publishing his book, Taki earned over $350,000 from his book in new high-ticket clients, group clients, and event ticket sales.

Shanda Sumpter wrote *Core Calling: How to Build a Business that Gives You a Freedom Lifestyle in Two Years or Less,* and earned over $400,000, generating 11,572 leads in just her first four months of using her book. She uses her book to sell her high-ticket coaching programs and, similar to Taki, to also attract people into her live event, which I've had the honor and privilege to speak at multiple times.

Our client Rob Nixon, who wrote *The Wealthy Accountant: How Accountants Can Earn More Than $1 Million in Profit While Working Less Than 500 Hours,* uses his books along with a cold email strategy to attract new clients into his business. In the very first week of launching his book he earned $90,000 from new clients.

PR & Media

Most people don't think of using PR and media to actually make money, but we've seen this as a very effective strategy for our clients. In fact, about seven years ago, it was so effective that we decided to build our own in-house PR team to get myself and our clients on TV and radio all over the United States and Canada. We now have clients appearing on media every single week.

> *Most people don't think of using PR and media to actually make money, but we've seen this as a very effective strategy for our clients.*

Our client Natasha Haslett wrote *Unstoppable Influence,* and we booked Natasha on TV throughout the southern United States. She wrote to us, "I just want to thank Rob and Liz for all your help. I actually have a meeting with Hay House next week, and a lot of it is due to your help in getting great PR and bestseller status for my book." Natasha was able to attract a traditional publisher deal simply because of her book's success with getting her on TV and radio.

Our client Kathy Heshelow, who wrote a book on anti-aging, was able to land a spread in *Lucky Magazine* viewed by more than over a million subscribers and sold over $100,000 in her products on Amazon in one month, simply because her book got her featured in *Lucky Magazine*.

RAISING MONEY

Doug Bowman and John Mullen used their book *Florencia: An Accidental Story* to start a successful nonprofit. In the first six months, they raised over $250,000 for their brand-new charity, got connected to the President of Mozambique (who wrote a new foreword for their book), and addressed the General Assembly of the United Nations, which I was also invited to. All this was accomplished by using their best-selling book to open the right doors.

My client Amir Baluch does it for a different reason. Amir is an anesthesiologist and avid real estate investor. He and many of his doctor friends have invested in real estate together and done well. Amir wanted to grow this into a business, helping doctors secure their retirement with real estate, but could never seem to raise money outside of his direct sphere of influence. So, we helped him launch his best-selling book, *Make It, Keep It: The New Rules of Wealth Preservation for Doctors.*

Amir began mailing his book to groups and associations (and individuals) of doctors and setting appointments to discuss what he does. Within the first six months of using the book, Amir raised over $2 million for real estate investing. Not a bad side hustle.

SPEAKING ENGAGEMENTS

Many authors want to use their book to attract speaking engagements, both online and offline. Our client Erica Ormsby, who wrote *I Am Happy. Healthy. Free: How to Become the Person Who Lives Your Dreams,* booked herself on her own speaking tour, going from Los Angeles to New York. She earned over

$39,000 on her speaking engagements over a period of about three months though she had never actually spoken and sold her programs from the stage before.

Amy Dix, who wrote *Seven More Days: Live a Life That's Bursting with Positivity and Happiness,* decided that after leaving her corporate job and selling her branding and design business, she wanted to be a paid speaker. Over a period of 18 months, Amy used her books and attracted 98 paid speaking arrangements, ranging from $5,000 to $12,000, as well as selling her books and her coaching. She went from never having earned a speaker fee to over a million dollars in speaker fees, all using her best-selling book.

Today, Amy and I are actually in business together in another company called Authority Speakers Agency, where we help our clients to do exactly what Amy did: land stages and speaking opportunities, either for a fee or to sell their coaching, courses, and products.

COURSES, PRODUCTS, AND SOFTWARE

Many people wouldn't think you'd be able to sell courses, products, or even software with a book. But that's exactly what our client Russell Brunson has done as he's built ClickFunnels into a billion-dollar company. Russell's books, *DotCom Secrets,* *Expert Secrets,* and *Traffic Secrets,* are used every day to educate people on the use of funnels and his software, in particular, ClickFunnels.

I watched Russell build this business from the beginning, using his books, and we were honored to be able to help him launch his very first book, *DotCom Secrets to Bestseller Status.* I'm also featured in Russell's book *30 Days,* which he uses as well to sell ClickFunnels and his software.

> *Book funnels are a tremendous way to attract new clients into your business, and in fact, it's the very thing that I'll be using with this book to sell my software, Manuscriptr.*

Book funnels are a tremendous way to attract new clients into your business, and in fact, it's the very thing that I'll be using with this book to sell my software, Manuscriptr.

Russell Brunson

Virtual Workshops/Challenges

Lastly, using your book to fill your virtual challenges and workshops is a very common strategy and one that we at Best Seller Publishing use very successfully.

Our past client Pedro Adao helped me do my very first challenge the month after the pandemic hit in April of 2020. That challenge, which I named *Publish. Promote. Profit.* after my book, helped us earn almost half a million dollars in new clients simply by using the content from my book. We also used the book to fill the workshop.

My client Gina Lester, who wrote *College Admissions Secrets*, went through our training on challenges for authors that Pedro and I put together, and here's what she had to say: "*I am overwhelmed with emotions. My book has opened so many doors. Not only am I an international bestseller, but I am now in the profit stage. Rob Kosberg helped me restructure my business model, and I just closed the cart on my first-ever challenge. This is where I open the doors to my group coaching, and the results: over $16,000 in sales. Guys, your book is your golden ticket, and having this team to support you is a huge blessing. Thank you, Best Seller Publishing.*" Gina went on to earn over $100,000 using her book and virtual challenges to attract clients into her new coaching business.

What if you were 1 Book Away?

College Admissions Secrets: Your
Teen's Unique Game Plan To ACE
Their Applications and Get Into Their
Dream school
by Dr. Gena Lester
★★★★⯪ · 25
Paperback
$24⁹⁵

Gena Lester
August 7, 2020 · 😊

I am overwhelmed with emotions. My book has opened so many doors. Not only am I an international best seller but I am now in the profit stage. Rob Kosberg helped me restructure my business model. I just closed the cart on my first ever challenge. This was where I opened the doors to my group coaching membership and the results....Over 16k in sales. Guys your book is your Golden ticket and having this team to support you is a huge blessing Thank you Best Seller Publishing!!

👍💙 You, Randy Taylor, Amy Dix and 21 others   16 Comments

❤ Love   💬 Comment

As I said, this is not an exhaustive study on Million Dollar Author strategies, but it's important that you see that ordinary people are doing extraordinary things using their books. Your book can make you six figures or even seven figures, even if it only sells a few hundred or a few thousand copies. You just need the right Million Dollar Author strategy.

By the way, as I am sure you can imagine Suze Orman has done quite well for herself, but primarily not from royalties and selling books. She has published 10 books and sold many (hundreds of thousands) copies, though exact figures are not known. Her net worth, however, is approaching $100,000,000 and she has done that by impacting tens of millions of people on TV and media. Not a bad Million Dollar Author strategy, I'd say.

If you'd like a free training on how to use your book to get on TV and media like we help our clients do, then go to https://publishmybestseller.com/robsgiveaway

CONCLUSION

Elizabeth was going through a difficult divorce. Like many in that situation, she was lost, confused, and seeking solace. After her divorce, she decided to embark on a year-long journey around the world, hoping to find herself again. She traveled to Italy, India, and Indonesia. In Italy, she explored the pleasures of food and language. In India, she immersed herself in spirituality and meditation. And in Indonesia, she found love and balance.

During her travels, she decided to write and document her experiences, thoughts, and feelings. She thought it could be a book. Elizabeth Gilbert's book *Eat, Pray, Love* became a global bestseller, translated into over 30 languages and selling 12 million copies. It was later adapted into a film starring Julia Roberts. The book resonated with millions of readers worldwide, many of whom were inspired to embark on their own journeys of self-discovery. Gilbert's story illustrates the power of writing a book. It's not just about telling a story; it's about sharing experiences, inspiring others, and making a difference.

After her success, she was asked, "Why did you want to write a book?" Her answer was simple yet profound. She wanted to share her journey of self-discovery and healing with others who might be going through similar struggles. She wanted to inspire and give hope.

Truth be told, I haven't read the book or seen the movie; I'm probably missing out. But millions of people have and have been impacted by it and her writing.

I don't know if your book could have that kind of impact or not. I do know that it CANNOT if you never write it.

I feel as though I have unlocked a super power or perhaps a super short cut.

I have written this book from start to finish in a long weekend. I've never done that before, not even close. I feel as though I have unlocked a super power or perhaps a super short cut. I have done my best to pass it on to you and I hope you will write your book. For yourself, your business, your legacy, and your reader.

I will be passing this manuscript over to my team in the next 30 minutes for design, formatting, and publishing and I will have a physical copy in my hand in the next couple of weeks.

To learn more about Manny, go to:
https://publishmybestseller.com/ai-workshop